How we **USE** materials

Rocks
and
Stones

Rita Storey

A⁺
Smart Apple Media

This book has been published in cooperation with Franklin Watts.

Series designed and created for Franklin Watts by Painted Fish Ltd., Art Director: Jonathan Hair, Designer: Rita Storey, Editor: Fiona Corbridge

Picture credits:
Corbis/Peter Beck p. 24, p. 18 (bottom); istockphoto.com p. 6, p. 7, p. 8, p. 9, p. 10, p. 11, p. 12, p. 13, p. 14, p. 15, p. 16, p. 17, p. 18 (top), p. 19 (top), p. 20, p. 21, p. 22, p. 23 (top), p. 25, p. 27 (top); Tudor Photography p. 18 (bottom), p. 19 (bottom), p. 26, p. 27 (bottom); www.holloways.co.uk p. 23 (bottom).

Cover images: Tudor Photography, Banbury; www.holloways.co.uk (bottom).

Published in the United States by Smart Apple Media
2140 Howard Drive West, North Mankato, Minnesota 56003

Library of Congress Cataloging-in-Publication Data

Storey, Rita.
Rocks and stones / by Rita Storey.
p. cm. – (How we use materials)
Includes index.
ISBN-13: 978-1-59920-006-4
1. Rocks—Juvenile literature. 2. Stone—Juvenile literature. 3. Building materials—Juvenile literature. I. Title.

QE432.2.S77 2007
552—dc22   2006029885

9 8 7 6 5 4 3 2 1

Contents

Words in **bold** are
in the glossary.

5

What are rocks and stones?

Rock is a **natural material** that is found above and below the ground. Stones are small pieces of rock.

There are rocky cliffs and mounds of rock above the ground. People like to climb them.

Large pieces of rock are called boulders and are very hard and heavy.

The wind, rain, and frost break down rocks to make stones. Stones that have become smooth from rubbing against each other are called pebbles.

Sand is often made of millions of tiny pieces of rock. Each piece is called a grain.

Sand feels soft when you touch it. You play with it on the beach and in sandboxes.

Rock keywords
Natural
Boulder
Pebble
Sand

Where do rocks come from?

It takes millions of years to make rock. There is a layer of rock around Earth. It is called the crust. There are many different kinds of rock.

Some rocks, such as pumice, came from **volcanoes**. Pumice is a very light rock. It is full of holes made by bubbles of air. Pumice stones can be rubbed on skin to keep it smooth.

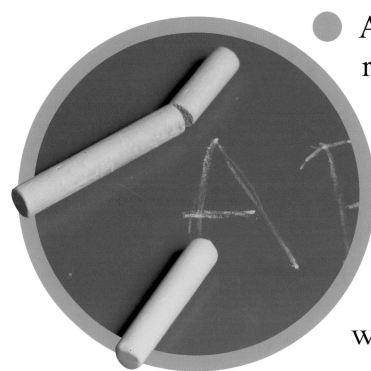

Another kind of rock is from the sea. Chalk is a very soft rock made from crushed seashells. It can be made into sticks and used for writing.

Some rocks, such as marble, were once a boiling liquid, which cooled and became solid. This kind of rock is very hard. Marble can be polished to make it shine.

Rock keywords
Pumice
Chalk
Marble

Mines and quarries

Rock is a very useful material because it is hard and strong. We get rock from **mines** and **quarries**.

Some rock is deep under the ground. People have to dig to get it out. This is called mining.

When rock on the surface or in hillsides is cut away, it is called quarrying.

This rock in a quarry has been broken by **explosives**. The bits of rock are washed and sorted into different sizes.

Rock keywords

Mines
Quarries
Explosives

The rock that comes from a quarry is called stone. Stone has to be cut using machines like this one.

Building materials

Rock is very strong and lasts for a long time. It is also waterproof. These things make rock a good building material.

● Blocks of stone can be used for the walls of buildings. Builders use different types of stone for their color and pattern.

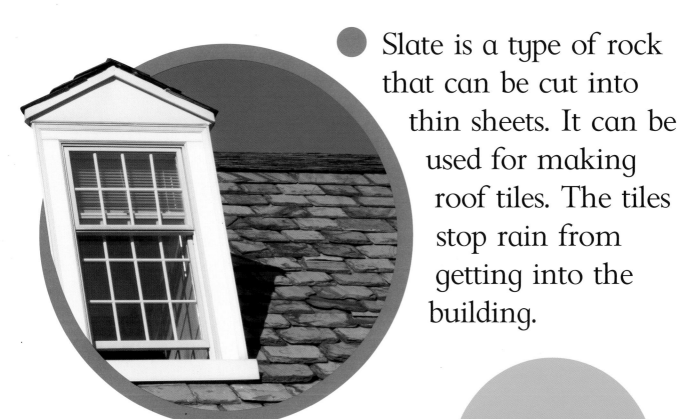

Slate is a type of rock that can be cut into thin sheets. It can be used for making roof tiles. The tiles stop rain from getting into the building.

Tiny pieces of rock are called gravel. Gravel is usually found in rivers or the sea. Some **driveways** are covered with gravel.

Rock keywords

Strong
Waterproof
Gravel

Cement and concrete

Cement and **concrete** are strong building materials that are made from rocks.

Cement is a mixture of crushed **limestone** and **clay**.

Builders mix cement with sand and water to make **mortar**. They use mortar to stick bricks together to make walls.

Concrete is an even stronger material made of cement, sand, gravel, and water. It is mixed in a concrete mixer like this one.

When the concrete is first mixed, it is a sticky paste. When it dries, it becomes very hard and strong.

We can make concrete objects in different shapes by pouring wet concrete into **molds** and letting it dry.

Rock keywords
Cement
Limestone
Mortar
Concrete

Building with concrete

All buildings need a firm base on the ground underneath them so that they do not fall down. This base is called the **foundation.**

Foundations are made from tough concrete.

Tall buildings are made of concrete because stone is too heavy.

Concrete can be made stronger by putting metal rods inside it. This is called **reinforced concrete**.

Rock keywords
Reinforced
Foundation
Polished

Concrete is gray and often rough. To make concrete buildings look nicer, thin sheets of colored stone are sometimes glued to the outside. This building is covered in sheets of polished marble.

17

At home

Rocks and stones are nice to look at and many are very **durable**.

● Some kitchens have **granite** countertops. Granite is a speckled rock. You can put hot pans on it and it will not burn. You can cut food on it and it will not get scratched.

● This hard stone pestle (stick) and mortar (bowl) are used to grind food into powder.

Floor tiles are often made of stone. Stone stays cool and helps keep houses cool in hot weather.

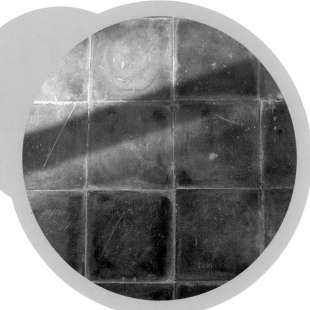

Stone is used for fireplaces because it does not burn.

Rock keywords
Cool
Beautiful
Durable
Granite

Marble is a beautiful rock. It is used for sinks, floors, chopping boards, and bowls.

In the street

Rocks and stones are very important for building roads because they are strong.

Roads need to be very durable so that they can support the weight of heavy trucks without **crumbling**.

They are made with a layer of large stones covered by a layer of smaller stones. Then a smooth layer of concrete or **asphalt** goes on top.

● Granite is a very hard stone. It is used to make the edges of sidewalks, or curbs. It lasts for a long time.

● Sidewalks are sometimes made from **slabs** of concrete. The slabs are very cheap to make.

● *Rock keywords*

Sidewalk
Hard
Slab
Cheap

In the garden

Rocks and stones have many different uses in the garden. We choose them because they are strong and waterproof and just because they look nice.

Gravel is used to make garden paths.

Garden seats are sometimes made of stone. They can be outside in all types of weather.

Rock keywords

Heavy

Stone is used to make **containers** for growing plants. Stone is heavy, so the containers are not blown over by the wind.

Rocks and stones in art

Rock can be cut, shaped, and polished. It is a good material for artists to use.

An artist can use sharp tools to chip away at a block of stone to make a shape. This is called a sculpture.

An artist who does this is called a sculptor.

Marble is often used for making sculptures because it has beautiful patterns and it can be polished to make it shine.

Rock keywords

Cut

Shape

Polish

Mosaic

In **Roman times,** artists made **mosaic** floors from small pieces of stone. They used different colors to make patterns and pictures of people and animals.

Gemstones

Precious stones called gemstones can be found inside some rocks.

● When gemstones are cut and polished, they sparkle, so they make beautiful jewelry, such as this ring.

Some gemstones are very expensive because they are difficult to find.

● Some gemstones are easier to find and less expensive. They are polished and made into jewelry.

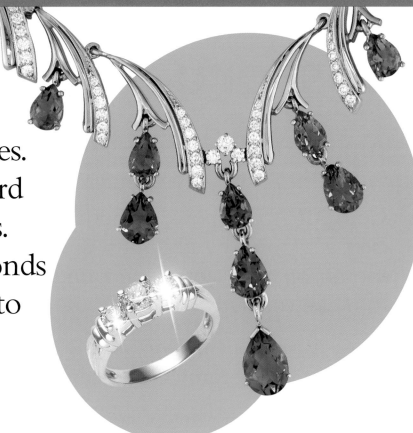

Diamonds

are gemstones. They are hard and colorless. Large diamonds are made into jewelry.

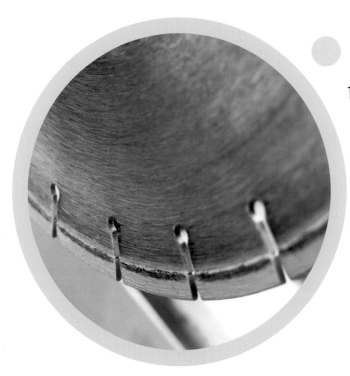

Small diamonds are used to cut with. They are used on the edges of knives and saws. The blade of this saw has tiny diamonds on it. It can cut through metal.

Rock keywords

Gemstone
Diamond

Glossary

Asphalt A substance made from oil that is used as a surface on roads.

Cement A fine powder made of limestone and clay. It is mixed with water and sand to make mortar or with water, sand, and small stones to make concrete.

Clay A type of fine earth which can be used to make bricks, ceramics, and cement.

Concrete A mixture of cement, water, sand, and small stones. It is used to build with.

Containers Objects, such as cartons, cans, jars, or boxes, used for holding or carrying things.

Crumbling Breaking up.

Diamond A colorless gem. Diamonds are the hardest rocks.

Driveway A hard path for a car that goes from the street to a house.

Durable Something that is strong and lasts a long time.

Explosives Substances used to blow up things into little bits; they make a loud noise.

Foundation The base beneath a building.

Granite A very hard rock with a speckled pattern that comes in different colors.

Limestone A white rock used to make cement.

Mines Holes dug in the ground to get rocks and minerals.

Mortar A mixture of cement, sand, and water that is used to stick bricks or stones together. It hardens when it is dry.

Mosaic A picture or design made from small colored pieces of stone or tile attached to a surface.

Molds Containers in special shapes, into which liquids can be poured. When a liquid cools in a mold, it becomes a solid in the shape of the mold.

Natural material Something that comes from the earth, plants, or animals.

Quarries Places where stone is dug from the ground.

Reinforced concrete Concrete made stronger by adding metal rods.

Roman times A time in history about 2,000 years ago, when the Romans, a people from Italy, ruled a large part of the world.

Slabs Thick pieces of something.

Volcanoes Openings in Earth's crust through which very hot liquid rock, called lava, can flow.

Index